Scru

How to Leverage User Stories For Better Requirements Definition

By Jefferson Hanley

Table of Contents

SECTION I 4
1.0 INTRODUCTION 4
   1.1 About This Book 4
   1.2 About User Stories 6
   1.3 Who Should Read This Book 8

SECTION II 10
2.0 USER STORIES - The Basics 10
   2.1 Evolution of User Requirements Definition 10
   2.2 User Stories - Compared & Contrasted 20
   2.3 Role of User Stories in Projects 24

SECTION II 30
3.0 User Stories - Pros/Cons 30
   3.1 Why User Stories? 30
   3.2   Why NOT User Stories? 33
   3.3 Should We...Or Shouldn't We? 34

SECTION II 37
4.0 Hypothetically speaking 37
   4.1 Illustrative Building Blocks 37
   4.2 Linking Building Blocks to The Basics 42

SECTION III 45
5.0 The Rules 45
   5.1 Introductory Principles of User Stories 45
   5.2 Rules Explained 51
   5.3 How Rules Help Build User Stories 54

SECTION III 57
6.0 Acceptance Criteria 57
   6.1 Reminder: Why User Stories Were Written 57
   6.2 How Are They Validated? 59
   6.3 Why Acceptance Criteria? 61

Copyrights: Axellerata Publishing, 2015 ©

  6.4 What Do They Look Like?.. 62

SECTION III 65
7.0 The Approach 65
7.1 Using The Right Approach 65
7.2 User Story Techniques 71

SECTION III 77
8.0 Impact of US on Agile Projects 77
8.1 Using User Stories in Agile Projects 77
8.2 User Story Lifecycle 81

SECTION III 89
9.0 Doing it right - Tips & Tricks 89
9.1 Why Do It Right? 89
9.2 How To Do It Right? 92

SECTION IV 98
10.0 Samples & Examples 98
10.1 Introducing the Salesperson 99
10.2 The Salespersons' Stories 100
10.2.2 User Story 002.00 - Customer History Look-up................. 106
10.2.3 User Story 002.A & B - Customer Order/Payment History Look-up 108
10.3 The End Of Storytelling 112

SECTION IV 114
11.0 Tools & Products 114
11.1 Useful Links 114
11.2 Disclaimer 116

Copyrights: Axellerata Publishing, 2015 ©

SECTION I

1.0 INTRODUCTION

1.1 About This Book

This book has been written not just to provide new comers into the Project Management arena and existing veterans some great insight into User Stories; but it also helps everyone understand how User Stories can be leveraged to provide a great project experience for everyone - Project Sponsors, Project Financers, End Users, and most importantly the Project Team.

I've used my experience working with User Stories to highlight my Define, Refine, Consign and Combine approach to User Stories. By following this approach, both expert and newbie PM's will learn how to leverage User Stories to:

- Define user requirements at a very high level

- Refine them by drilling down into further detail
- Consign them to a central part of scoping a project
- Combine them with other tools to make project management more effective

While the information provided here will certainly benefit PM's that follow ANY project management methodology to deliver projects in ANY discipline, the focus of the content here is on Agile Project Management within an IT project environment. HOWEVER, I'll stress once again: What you learn from this book, about User Stories, can be easily adapted to make it relevant to projects in Engineering, Construction or any other discipline.

After you have finished reading this book, you will have a deep understanding of the importance that User Stories have in the life of an Agile project. You'll also equip yourself with an intimate knowledge of how to use them effectively as a project management tool.

Copyrights: Axellerata Publishing, 2015 ©

Combining this knowledge with that provided in other series of books, including *Project Management: A Compact Guide to the Complex World of Project Management*, and *Scrum: Your Quick Start Guide To Adopting Scrum For Your Organization*, will help you become a PM that delivers every project on time, within budget and to the highest of quality standards!

1.2 About User Stories

So, for the benefit of those unfamiliar with it, before you go any further, let me take just a few moments of your time to introduce you to the main character of this book: The User Story!

Remember, good Agile project management is all about collaboration, and documentation usually takes a back seat (though a very important one!). User Stories are therefore a way to use text narratives, to describe how a "User" (defined as anyone that uses or depends on the system being developed) collaborates and interacts with the system. It's really that simple!

If you understand that brief definition of User Stories, then you are all set to unlock the power that they have on your projects, and this book will provide you the keys to do so. In the event that you are still unsure about what User Stories are - don't worry! We'll be going into considerable details shortly.

For now, suffices it to say that a User Story is a tool that will help articulate, to project managers and system designers and application developers, what the user needs from the system. This book will highlight how best to help users discuss those stories, and illustrate ways in which to document and present them.

It is worth reiterating the concept (and place) of "documentation" in an Agile setting, especially when it comes to building User Stories. The phrase "text narratives" used earlier shouldn't be confused for multi-volume documents. On the contrary: When it comes to User Stories, and building narratives around them, "Less is more!". We'll go into more details later in the book.

This book will show you how to create User Stories that are succinct yet powerful and effective!

1.3 Who Should Read This Book

For those of us that are a bit 'long in the tooth' in the IT industry, User Stories might not be a new term. Many of us have used them from time to time during various projects that we may have undertaken. However, many new comers into the field, especially those breaking ground into Project Management, might not really be all that familiar with User Stories.

If you are in that camp, then this book has been written for you!

Over the last decade or so, the project management world has seen a dramatic shift towards embracing newer, and more efficient, project management methodologies. PM's have especially taken to the Agile methodology, since it offers an ideal blend of rapid project deployment, while also balancing user requirements. Agile practitioners employ a number of tools to help define project scope and requirements, and User Stories are one such tool in their toolbox.

If you wish to learn how to use this tool more effectively, then this book is definitely for you!

If you have previously read other books in this series, including *Project Management: A Compact Guide to the Complex World of Project Management*, and *Scrum: Your Quick Start Guide To Adopting Scrum For Your Organization*, then you will already have a very strong foundation for understanding some of the theory and concepts that will be discussed here. If you haven't yet read those titles, I would strongly recommend them as great reading. HOWEVER, you will find the contents of this book of tremendous benefit, even if you use it as a "stand alone" guide.

Copyrights: Axellerata Publishing, 2015 ©

SECTION II

2.0 USER STORIES - The Basics

2.1 Evolution of User Requirements Definition

The formal definition of User Requirements (UR) might be thought of as evolving out of a sense of "paralysis" during the early days of computer software development.

- When teams of computer engineers got together to develop an application system, they knew exactly how to code and how to design and develop the application, but they knew nothing about how the business process worked!
- This in turn lead to the idea that business experts, who would ultimately use the systems, should lead the development

process. But when groups of business process specialists worked together to try and build the application, they found themselves restricted by lack of knowledge about the development and coding process!

Although both teams were highly skilled in their own respective disciplines, it lead to an environment of paralysis:

- Paralysis by over analysis, when business people designed computer systems
- Paralysis by lack of analysis, when computer specialists tried to engineer business applications

In the late 50's and early 60's, when mainframe computers broke out of the sheltered military domain, and started to become more ubiquitous in supporting business processes, there was an acute understanding that this paralysis could hinder the ability of computers in helping businesses run efficiently. As a result, formal system design and development methodologies evolved, which aided in the definition of user requirements.

2.1.1 Traditional User Requirements Definition

User Requirement definition was traditionally thought of as being a set of criteria that systems have to adhere to. Since most traditional applications were business process oriented, traditional URs were defined as the capabilities, constraints and conditions that were imposed on the application.

Traditional URs conformed to the following standards:

- Presentation: They were almost always expressed in textual form, with no room for graphical expressions
- Perspective: They were always written from a business perspective rather than the application point of view

- Comprehensive: They were written in as much specificity as possible, leaving no open ended requirements embedded in them
- Specific: Each requirement had to be very specific. There was no room for unambiguous statements
- Test capable: The requirements had to be such that they could be tested by the system developers

The focus of traditional URs was to define how the system was expected to operate. As such, they were deliberately written by concatenating scores of "shall" statements to form the basis of the requirements: For instance:

- The system shall only accept numbers between 1 and 10,000 in this field
- The system shall display the following message if the above requirement is violated "Incorrect number range entered"
- etc...

Since traditional UR were often "written in stone", they were developed to be extremely formal and rigid, much like a legal document would. The objective was to "nail them down" before coding could commence.

2.1.2 Use Cases

As system designing and development methodologies matured, a new way of defining URs evolved called the Use Case.

Use Cases documented a sequence of interactions that a User (referred to as an Actor) had with the system, and the resultant response that the system delivered. Unlike the traditional URs, which were solely text-based, Use Cases are split into two components:

- **Use Case Diagrams:** These are graphical representations of the Use Case, and they described what the Use Case was about, who the main Actors were, what the system boundaries were (with respect to the data required/used by the Use Case), and what relationships existed between these three components (Use Case, Actors and Boundaries)

- **Use Case Description:** This is a narrative of the Use Case, but was much less restrictive and more expressive than the simple "shall" statements used in traditional URs. They are written in a way that describes an action that a user would perform on/with the system (a Call), and how the system should react (Response) when it got that Call

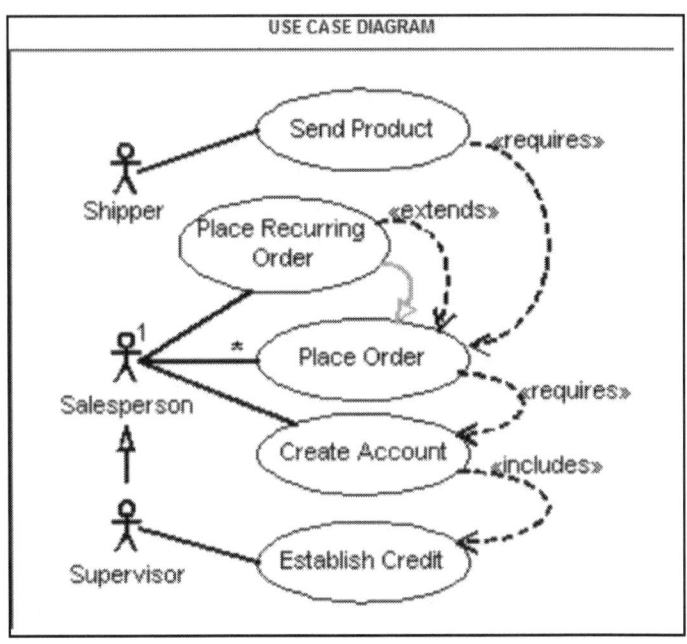

Use Case ID:	[Repeat for multiple use cases]		
Use Case Name:			
Created By:		Last Updated By:	
Date Created:		Last Revision Date:	
Actors:			
Description:			
Trigger:			
Preconditions:			
Postconditions:			
Normal Flow:			
Alternative Flows:			
Exceptions:			
Includes:			
Frequency of Use:			
Special Requirements:			
Assumptions:			
Notes and Issues:			

In the above instance, Shipper, Sales Person and Supervisor are various Actors that interact with the system. And for each of those interactions, a Use Case would be defined highlighting what behaviour would trigger what response from the system. Amongst other attributes of this interaction between Actors and System, the textual part of the Use Case would also define what the "Normal" response would be, and how "Exceptions" should be dealt with.

2.1.3 User Stories - What they are?

Which finally brings us to the subject of this book - User Stories!

So what exactly are User Stories, and how did they evolve?

Well, as the world of system design and development opened up, application users and system developers realized one very important fact:

The reason that they are building the system is so that it can make life for the User (and not necessarily the Developer) easier!

This recognition changed how URs were viewed, creating a whole new paradigm of how they were developed. The User-centric nature of system development now meant that URs too had to be gathered with that focus in mind. While the central idea behind the new way of capturing URs remained the same as that of Use Cases, in that the new approach still defined the interaction between User and System; the focus of those interactions however changed dramatically.

The new focus was now on what <u>value</u> the system delivers to the User!

And the best way, in which user requirement documenters found they could establish this new focus, was to define requirements in terms of metaphors. As a result, User Stories were born!

Without really going into details at this point in the book (more to follow), User Stories seek to

---

Copyrights: Axellerata Publishing, 2015 ©

metaphorically define each requirement by articulating them in the following form:

> **User Story Template**
> As a [user role]
> I want to [desired feature]
> so that [value/benefit]

SOURCE:Kasperspiro.com

- **User Role:** Which specifies in what capacity the user wishes to interact with the system - e.g. Shipper, Salesperson, Supervisor
- **Desired Feature:** Which describes, at a very high-level, what the particular role wishes to accomplish - e.g. Ship product, Place an order, Establish credit
- **Value Proposition:** This is where the focus is highlighted on the value generated from the User Story - e.g. "I can invoice the customer"; "Delivery schedules are met"

By speaking in metaphors, the User Story focuses on the work that the system should be doing for the user, and not on specific "features" that must be built into the system. And this refocusing of UR definition meshed well the modern concepts of Agile development, where the focus is not on the documentation created by the UR definition process, but rather on the need for multiple roles to collaborate when developing a particular User Story.

2.2 User Stories - Compared & Contrasted

This then begs the question: How do User Stories really differ from the other forms of UR definition?

Well, recapping from our earlier discussions, we see that there are several areas where User Stories differ from the other forms of capturing user requirements. Firstly, and most importantly, is the focus that a particular UR definition tool has:

- With Traditional UR definition, we saw that the focus was on system features, and what operational capabilities would be built into the system
- With Use Cases, they are written from the perspective of the interaction between Actors and the System
- User Stories on the other hand focus on the value that the particular story brings to the user, without greatly trying to define the way in which the system should deliver that value

The second differentiating aspect of the three UR definition approaches lies in the way they are defined:

- Traditionally, user requirements are outlined using very specific text, with the intent of eliminating any misinterpretations in what they are saying

- Use Cases are produced using a combination of graphics and text, and provide a fair bit of detail about a particular requirement. This matching of text with graphical techniques is intended to highlight Actor-System interactions
- User Stories on the other hand are not supposed to be too detailed or precise in their definition. They are therefore defined as metaphors for what's required, and NOT to spec out in detail what's actually required

Yet another difference between the three methods would be in who authors the UR:

- Traditionally, UR definition was the responsibility of the Business Analyst, who then worked with the System's Analyst to produce a System's Design Document (SDD) based on a User Requirements Document (URD)
- Use Cases are a bit more "technical" in nature, and require a higher degree of

technical expertise to create and understand. They are usually produced by the application design team, who have a fair degree of knowledge about "meta data" and systems flow of the application being created

- User Stories, on the other hand, are primary the responsibility of the Agile Product Owner (usually a representative of the end user). However, good Agile Project Management practices suggest that User Stories be created collaboratively between users and the technical teams. More on this aspect later!

Within an Agile project, User Stories undergo a series of transformations, in terms of the details they may contain. As noted earlier, User Stories, in an Agile context, are NOT supposed to document a particular system behaviour or characteristic. Rather, they are meant to serve as a "place holder" on the project's To-Do list that says:

This User Story is something we need to collaboratively have a conversation about - when we get to developing system functionality that addresses it!

As such, User Stories are a central ingredient of the Agile backlog management process, that gradually (over several Sprints and Iterations) see the complete system evolving.

2.3 Role of User Stories in Projects

Make no mistake: User Stories are NOT the same as Use Cases! The compare/contrast discussions above should have made that abundantly clear. However, unlike the more "meaty and fleshy" Use Cases, User Stories are not built (at least initially!) to deliver Agile project team's all of the information required to produce Scrum deliverables that rely of the User Story.

So, the question often arises: Do Agile project teams need to develop Use Cases in addition to a User Story. Not necessarily! Over the lifecycle of the project, the Scrum process evolves to organically put more meat on the bones of User Stories, and that eliminates the necessity of creating Use Cases.

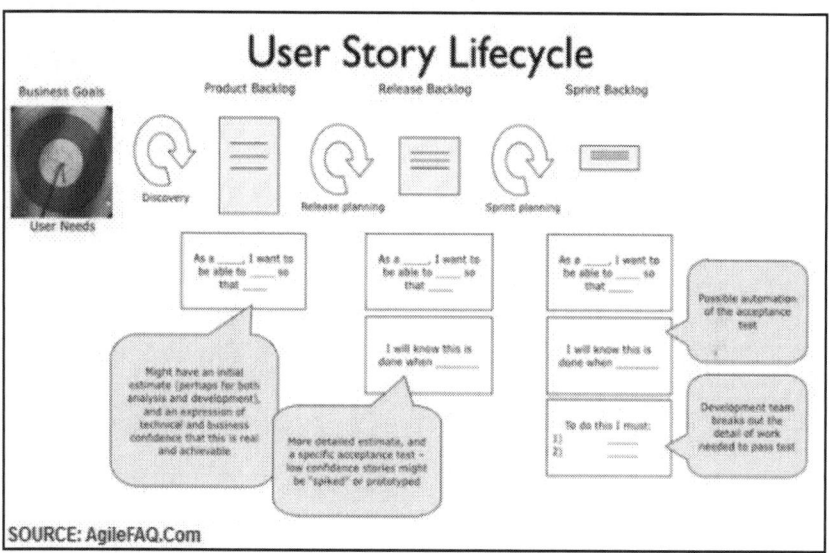

Agile practitioners will recall that, at its very basic, the Backlog Management Process is all about creating, updating and managing a "To Do" list of User Stories during every iteration of the project. At its very core, User Stories are place holders for the project team to remember to deliver a certain value-add for the Product Owner.

Copyrights: Axellerata Publishing, 2015 ©

During the life of an Agile project, each Sprint and every Release is made up of a collection of User Stories that the project team prioritizes and focuses its attentions upon. The role of these User Stories is therefore to bring forward a reminder that the entire project team - not just the Product Owner or Scrum Master - must collaborate to successfully deliver that value-add.

At the start of a project, the project team compiles the Product Backlog, which is a collection of User Stories that make up the entire universe of value (features, functionality, capabilities) that the Product Owner is looking for the project to deliver. This is the start of a series of conversations that must now take place, as part of the Product Planning cycle.

Next, during Release Planning, a sub-set of those User Stories (from the Product Backlog) are carved out, prioritized and presented as the Release Backlog. During the Release Planning process, additional conversations are held around each

User Story, gradually adding even more flesh to the skeleton User Story presented during Product Planning.

When the team next collaborates, during Sprint Backlog Planning, a subset of the User Stories (prioritized during the Release Planning process) are carved out of the Release Backlog and included into the Sprint Backlog. This small To Do list now becomes the focus of delivery for the ensuing project Sprint. And as the team works to deliver its Sprint commitments, even more clarity is sought (and received) about each of the User Stories they must work on.

The role of User Stories in an Agile project is therefore:

- **Product Planning:** To initially capture the ideal requirement that a user may perceive, and assess whether it is "doable" or technically sound

- **Release Planning:** To then further review that requirement, and build additional details around it, including how it's delivery will be tested/accepted (more on Acceptance criteria/testing later)
- **Sprint Planning:** To further breakdown the requirement into smaller work steps needed to finally deliver the User Story

The role of the User Story is NOT to provide all of the information components right off the bat. Instead, it is a tool to be used during projects to foster discussion, collaboration and debate about user requirements. As the project moves through its lifecycle, the User Stories that will be delivered by the project also pass through their own lifecycle, evolving during the process. This is the classic Define and Refine process we introduced earlier on in the book.

For a more in-depth discussion on this topic, readers may find it useful to refer to a previous publication - *Scrum: Your Quick Start Guide To Adopting Scrum For Your Organization*.

Copyrights: Axellerata Publishing, 2015 ©

SECTION II

3.0 User Stories - Pros/Cons

Given what we now know about User Stories, the question that many novice (and veteran!) Project Managers might ask is: Why should we use User Stories when other alternatives are available?

A legitimate counter question to that might be: Well, why NOT?

Let's briefly explore the answer to both these questions before we delve deeper into how User Stories are created.

3.1 Why User Stories?

As a way to gather user requirements, regardless of what project management methodology is followed to run the project, User Stories have proven extremely "handy". They are a particular tool of choice for requirements gathering on Agile projects, and that's where their utility has come to be greatly valued.

Here are some answers to the question: Why should we use User Stories?

- Unlike many of its peer user requirement documenting tools, User Stories approach requirements from a users' perspective. Most other tools take an application, product or system's approach to this process
- User Stories approach requirement definition using a very simple "As a..", "I want..", "So that I can.." role-based approach. This then forces "techies" on the project to step out of their "technical solution" delivery mode, and start to think in terms of "real world" solutions
- User Stories are succinct in their content, which allows the team to focus on discrete functionality, without initially getting bogged down in the myriad of details of the solution-to-be

- Unlike Use Cases, which contain a lot of technical graphic/pictorial depictions of the requirements, User Stories can be produced and understood by anyone on the team
- User Stories are primarily used as a tool to remind the entire team (not just the Architects or the Developers) that collaboration needs to happen about a particular User Story. This means that the ultimate solution will be one that's "owned" by everyone, and NOT enforced by the technical designers on the team
- By its very process, User Story creation is iterative in nature, which means each Story is enhanced and fleshed out through the Product, Release and Sprint processes. On the other hand, requirements in many other approaches are "nailed tight", with little or no chance of updates/changes as the design and development process unfolds
- User Stories are always transparently displayed for everyone on the project team to view and

access. Many other technical documents, such as Use Cases, are too verbose and unwieldy to post on a whiteboard (like User Stories are)

With all of this going for them, User Stories are definitely a force to be reckoned with when it comes to capturing user requirements.

3.2   Why NOT User Stories?

For all their advantages, User Stories are sometimes not looked upon favourably by some project management practitioners and project sponsors. Here's why:

- User Stories are construed as being extremely "thin" on content, and may be hard to create for project teams who are not accustomed to using them
- When defining requirements for complex process-oriented tasks, User Stories might not be the best tool to use. Many PMs prefer to see a lot of documentation and supplemental notes when it comes to such tasks, and are skeptical

of requirements articulated on 5x3 inch post it notes!

- And that brings us to yet another criticism of User Stories, which is that they don't "look or feel" like a requirement document at all...more like a collection of random thoughts scribbled on post it paper.

All of these are legitimate concerns that project management professionals should take into consideration when deciding whether to use User Stories.

3.3 Should We...Or Shouldn't We?

While the final determination, on whether to use or not to use User Stories, should rightly be left to individual project teams, the biggest plus for using them - Collaboration - should not be ignored:

User Stories force project teams to look at requirements in terms of "Who" and "Why", rather than the "What"!

Technical team members collaborating in the development of the User Story then use that information, to hash out the "How".

For individuals associated with the project that want additional or supplemental information about specific user requirements, there's no hard and fast rule that such details cannot (should not or will not!) be produced. From an Agile project management framework, User Stories are what drives the process efficiently. However, when and if required, additional information can definitely be gathered about requirements, and articulated in any form that the team feels comfortable using.

Since the end objective of most projects is to deliver value-add to a user, it is only fair (and logical!) therefore that the focus of the end product be the User who will benefit from the product. Traditional user requirement gathering processes, however, stray away from that concept. User Stories empower the end-user into making his/her voice heard when it comes to user requirements.

Copyrights: Axellerata Publishing, 2015 ©

SECTION II

4.0 Hypothetically speaking

So far, we've discussed many theoretical aspects of User Stories. It's high time that we now got into discussing them for REAL! In a subsequent part of the book (**Section IV Chapter 10.0 Samples & Examples**) we'll be building upon our discussions here, by taking a look at several examples of User Stories. For the purpose of our immediate discussions however, we'll use a hypothetical reference to a User Story to introduce you to a "real" User Story.

4.1 Illustrative Building Blocks

In a post, way back in 2001, Ron Jefferies provided some great insight into User Stories with his now famous "3C's" theory:

- Cards

- Conversation
- Confirmation

In many ways, these are the building blocks for creating great User Stories.

As an illustration, let's say a user (Shipper) wanted you to build an App to enter product shipments for the company. Here's how this hypothetical requirement might be developed into a User Story using the building block approach:

- **Card(s):** The Agile Product owner will write out the requirements on Cards (or perhaps on 5x3 inch Post-it pads). Essentially, what the Card will contain is a high-level requirement, and a description of why it is needed.

    The Shipper may say "As a Shipper, I want to be able to enter detailed information about Order Shipments quickly, so that the goods can be shipped out quickly"

    This is not meant to "document" the users' requirement, but instead just as a tool to identify that a specific requirement exists and, at some point in time during the project lifecycle, must be addressed. These Cards (or other alternates) are used primarily for planning and tracking purposes, and not as a substitute for detailed documentation of user requirements.

- **Conversation(s):** When the project reaches that "point in time", the Product Owner, End User and Project Team will initiate a conversation about this particular User Story. In the hypothetical instance above, the conversations will center around:
  - why the Shipper is asking for this requirement, and
  - what does he/she seek to gain by having it.

Perhaps, other side-bar conversations may revolve around what if situations:

- What if you didn't have this particular feature? or
- What if you got what you want...but in some other way?

The Card has ensured that the story remains front and center on everyone's mind, and as a result, it is now time to discuss how the project team can add value for this particular users needs.

Conversations about the User Story may continue over several days or weeks, and might even be held over several stages of an Agile project, until the User Story is finally scheduled for development.

- **Confirmation(s):** During the conversations, product designers, developers and testers will seek clarification about how "success" will be measured, once the requirements have been accommodated into the product by the developers. The intent is to get a clear-cut understanding of how the user will confirm that the project team has done what the User Story asks of them.

The project team could (hypothetically speaking) ask the Shipper:

- what information he/she needed the App to capture
- what calculations needed to be done
- how "quickly" does the data need to be processed
- what warnings/error messages need to be displayed

Without this third "C", no one on the team will know when the requirement has been developed, and neither will the user know if he/she has received it upon product delivery.

As we can see, putting all these 3C's together, we can gradually come up with pretty effective real-life User Stories.

4.2 Linking Building Blocks to The Basics

In an earlier part of this book *(Section II Chapter 2.0 User Stories - The Basics)*, we introduced you to some User Story basics, and explained their evolution and use. So let's now revisit some of those basics to see how the 3C building blocks discussed above fit in with our earlier discussions.

Back then (*refer to section 2.1.3*), we explained that one of the purposes of a User Story was to "...*metaphorically define each requirement*". We also introduced the User Story Template as a way to capture User Stories. Well, that "template" is actually the first of the building blocks - the Card - highlighted in our most recent discussions.

Previously, during that same discussion, we also identified that the User Story Template (or Card) should identify the User Role, the Desired Feature, and the Value Proposition. Those were the basics, and they tie in neatly with our current discussion about the building blocks only containing high-level requirements.

Again, during our earlier discussions we also spoke about one of the basic principles surrounding User Stories was *"...the need for multiple roles to collaborate when developing a particular User Story"*. That "collaboration" actually forms the second C of our building blocks - Conversation. In our discussions about the basics, we has said *"... good Agile Project Management practices suggest that User Stories be created collaboratively between users and the technical teams."*, and that's exactly what our building blocks underline here.

Our discussions of the basics also touched upon the fact that creating User Stories is an iterative process. We saw, from our discussions on the basics **(2.3 Role of User Stories in Projects)**, that a User Story might be discussed, reviewed and refined, during Product Planning, Release Planning and Sprint Planning.

Through each of these phases, the project team will try to get a more precise understanding of what the User Story entails. In doing so, they will be creating the third building block - Confirmation - of the User Story. Once they have a clear understanding of WHAT, they will define HOW it can be confirmed during testing. This Confirmation process is called "Acceptance Criteria", and we'll learn more about it in *Section II Chapter 6.0 Acceptance Criteria*.

SECTION III

5.0 The Rules

Now that we've taken a closer look at User Stories, albeit a bit hypothetically speaking, it's time to look at some "rules" that one needs to follow to make User Stories effective. The reason that we are using the word "rules" in quotes is because these are more of guiding principles than hard and fast commandments. They may even be looked at as best practices really.

5.1 Introductory Principles of User Stories

A key principle of building good User Stories is to start off with very broad statements, and then drill down into details as you go along. Think of the User Story Card (or Post It Note) as being a canvas placed before an artist. Most artists will never start painting the finer points of their picture immediately. They instead sketch out broad characteristics of the scenery first, and then gradually hone in on the specifics.

User Stories are no different.

5.1.1 Epics:

Most User Stories will often start with the definition of an Epic. These are often characterized as large stories that are often too vast in scope to implement in any given iteration. As a result, to be valuable to the project, an Epic will need to be decomposed further, into sub-User Stories before it can be prioritized in a backlog.

Usually, it is the smaller component User Stories that receive high priority during an iteration cycle. Why? Because they are easier to quantify, in terms of work effort and timelines involved to deliver them. As such, an Epic will usually end up receiving lower priority when the project team begins any backlog planning session.

In the case of our Shipping system analogy, an Epic might be:

> **"As a Salesperson, I want my customers to pay efficiently, so that I can collect my commissions quickly"**

Looking at such a User Story, it is hard (impossible actually!) to see exactly what this user is looking for. This story doesn't help the project team to quantify work requirements to deliver "efficiency", nor does it help them think of specifics on how to help the Salesperson get his/her commissions "quickly".

However, this Epic serves a very important purpose: It puts this user's requirement on the radar of the project team, and says that: At some point in time, we need to take this Epic apart and see what makes it tick!

One of the principles of dealing with Epics is not to rush out and immediately start decomposing every Epic into smaller User Stories. Doing so could

Copyrights: Axellerata Publishing, 2015 ©

needlessly end up burning scarce resources in accomplishing tasks that are not adding immediate value to the project. Instead, hold off making any commitment to decomposition of specific Epics until it's absolutely time to do so.

5.1.2 Themes

When an Epic (i.e. a "master story") is broken down into smaller User Stories, it can sometimes result in multiple stories that "belong" together. For instance, when the team gets together to have a conversation about the Salespersons Epic highlighted above, they might discover that, to fulfil this requirement, the team must cater for the following possibilities:

- Validate the customers' outstanding balance
- Allow credit limit verification against customer database
- Allow payment via Credit Card
- Allow payment via ApplePay
- Allow Payment via PayPal

In this case, the Epic has been broken down into 6 smaller User Stories related to two distinct Themes:

- **Theme#1:** Credit Checks:
    - User Story 1: Validate outstanding balance
    - User Story 2: Allow credit limit verification against customer database
- **Theme#2:** Payment Mode
    - User Story 3: Allow cash payment (in-store)
    - User Story 4: Allow payment via Credit Card
    - User Story 5: Allow payment via ApplePay
    - User Story 6: Allow Payment via PayPal

When Epics are broken down into smaller stories, it results in multiple User Stories that can be dealt with together, potentially in a single Release. The task of the project team is then simplified because they can focus on a group of related features/functionality at the same time. This decomposition, of Epics/Themes/User Stories, also helps assigning work to specialists that may have specific prior expertise/experience on working with similarly-grouped stories.

5.1.3 Planning Principles

Epics and Themes are a great way to prioritize Product, Release and Sprint backlogs with stakeholders and internal teams. Since some stakeholders prefer not to get too involved "in the weeds", they prefer to see project timelines and priorities defined in Epics - high-level; while others might like to see slightly more granularity in project plans and prioritization - lower-level.

For technical teams however, the most efficient way to prioritize backlogs is at the User Story level. That's because by then, Sprint Backlog Planning, detailed conversations will have taken place, lots of collaboration will have happened, and there will be much more clarity around what the needs are, and how to go about confirming (Acceptance Testing) the User Story.

5.2 Rules Explained

The "rules" (notice the small letters!) for User Stories are really very simple: They need to be easy to create, simple to understand, and effective in their use. This may sound too vague a "Rule" (caps!), and especially for newcomers to Agile, might not provide sufficient guidance when creating User Stories.

That's why, back in 2003, Bill Wake (one of the pioneers in Agile/XP methodology) coined an acronym to guide user requirement writers in producing effective User Stories.

Letter	Meaning	Description
I	Independent	The user story should be self-contained, in a way that there is no inherent dependency on another user story.
N	Negotiable	User stories, up until they are part of an iteration, can always be changed and rewritten.
V	Valuable	A user story must deliver value to the end user.
E	Estimable	You must always be able to estimate the size of a user story.
S	Scalable (small sized)	User stories should not be so big as to become impossible to plan/task/prioritize with a certain level of certainty.
T	Testable	The user story or its related description must provide the necessary information to make test development possible.

SOURCE: Wikipedia.Org

The INVEST methodology for producing User Stories can be construed as laying down the rules for producing User Stories within the Agile framework. Here's how various components of the acronym should be used:

- **Independent:** Ideally, each User Story should be written so that they are autonomous from each other. Creation of overlapping User Stories is highly discouraged because then, they might not be able to be scheduled (for development and implementation) independently.
- **Negotiable:** Earlier in our discussions (**Chapter 2**), we learned that, unlike conventional requirement definitions, User Stories are not contract-like. They have to be created through negotiation. The best User Stories are those which are born as a result of conversations amongst all stakeholders.
- **Valuable:** Simply put, any User Story that does not add value to the project is of no use! Conversely, a story that does have value, but that isn't presented as such, is not a good User Story.
- **Estimable:** A good User Story must be written in a way that the project team, tasked

with scheduling, designing and developing the underlying solution, can easily estimate the time and effort required to produce the solution. And that brings us to the next "rule"!

- **Scalable:** Agile Project teams usually like to keep Sprints to a maximum of 1 to 2 week durations. Therefore, User Stories must be written so that they can be completed within a Sprint timeframe. A story that requires more than this amount of effort is usually a story that's been poorly written.
- **Testable:** The final "rule" is that every User Story must be written with appropriate testing points to it. Recall our discussion from the previous chapter (**4.0 Illustrative Building Blocks**). The Testable requirement is derived from the third of our building blocks - Confirmation. If the User Story does not have an associated Acceptance Criteria (see **Chapter 6.0 Acceptance Criteria** for more

details), then it will not be of any value to the team.

If you follow these rules diligently, you are sure to be able to produce extremely effective User Stories.

5.3 How Rules Help Build User Stories

The next valid question would be: How do these "rules" really help us build effective User Stories? The answer is: By enforcing a structured discipline that we need to follow when creating them, we end up producing great User Stories.

As you go about building User Stories, ask yourself the questions:

- Does this User Story conform to my 3C building blocks?
- Is this story too detailed/verbose...do I need to break it up?
- Is this something that everyone agrees upon...or was it just forced upon the team?

- Does delivering what the story request make sense for the User?
- Can we even deliver what's being asked?
- And if it is something that can be delivered - is it something that can be produced during one Sprint (usually a week)
- Do we know how to test the User Story once it's been developed?

Once a team starts building User Stories, it is often difficult to immediately identify which ones are good, and which ones don't quite cut it. And unless there is a discipline built around writing them, User Stories can actually be a cause for project failure rather than success.

By carefully asking these questions for every User Story that comes into the Product, Release and Sprint backlog, Agile project teams can ensure that the story is firmly grounded to the rules of producing good User Stories. Think of the questions as a "check list" that every user story needs to pass, before it can be slotted for final development.

Make no mistake: No one is suggesting that when a User Story is first proposed, all of these rules MUST be assessed for compliance immediately. On the contrary, the very iterative process of building them means User Stories are never finished in one go. And because they are reviewed and refined over time, a quick check of the rules each time a refinement is made helps build better, usable User Stories.

Refer to **Section II Chapter 9.0 Getting it right - Tips & Tricks** for more on how to go about building good User Stories

SECTION III

6.0 Acceptance Criteria

Regardless of what development methodology is followed, Waterfall, JIT, Agile, one key element in the project lifecycle will always be Testing. And in order for a product, whether it's a train, a space ship or a software application, to be tested successfully, the tester (and the Product owner) must know what "success" will like once achieved.

Simply stated, a User Story's "Acceptance criteria" tells everyone what's needed to confirm that the story was delivered successfully.

6.1 Reminder: Why User Stories Were Written

Before we dive into the nuts and bolts of Acceptance criteria, it behoves us to reminder ourselves why we create User Stories in the first place. Recapping from earlier discussions, we know that the purpose of User Stories is to use metaphors to highlight a certain "want" or "need". And that's a great way to succinctly tell the project team, at a very high level, how they can add value for the product owner/user.

The problem with metaphors is that they are often very abstract in their description, lacking a lot of specifics. That's NOT a lacking on the part of User Stories - because that's EXACTLY how they are meant to be created. However, this does pose a conundrum for the developer:

- Should the developer insist on very detailed (and verbose) User Stories - so they (User Stories) can get a lot more specific? And the answer is - No! Because that defeats the purpose of using User Stories in Agile projects

And there lies the challenge for developers. How do they know that they have successfully delivered the value, as represented by the User Story, to the product owner/user?

It also poses a similar challenge to product owners/users: How do they validate that the value requested by a User Story has, in fact, been received?

6.2 How Are They Validated?

The simple answer to both of the preceding questions is: Through Acceptance criteria!

When a Product Owner/User launches the lifecycle of a User Story during the Product Planning process, he/she kicks off a series of discussions that would hypothetically occur as follows:

- Product Owner: Will describe what he/she needs from the project team
- Project Team: Will ask a series of questions, seeking additional clarification about what it is exactly that is needed
- Product Owner: Will elaborate, more explicitly, what's needed

- Project Team (Developers/Testers): Will probe further, to understand how they can build what the Product Owner/User is asking for
- Product Owner: Will supplement earlier information with more specifics, identifying more precisely how the tool should behave in order to satisfy him/her

As a result of this interactive, collaborative process, Developers and Testers will use what the Product Owner/User tells them, and translate it into words, phrases and sentences called Acceptance criteria.

During product development, the development team uses those criteria to test whether the tool actually does what the user requested. When the product (or sub-sections/sub-components of it) has been developed, the Product Owner will once again use those same Acceptance criteria to then validate if the product meets his/her requirement as outlined by the User Story.

6.3 Why Acceptance Criteria?

Acceptance criteria serve multiple purposes, for multiple players/roles on an Agile project.

- They help Developers/Testers to persevere in a line of questioning (of the Product owner) so that "actionable" information is gleaned from the owner/user, which can then be used to actually build product functionality
- They help Product Owners/Users think more substantially about the requirements they are requesting from the project team
- They serve as a catalyst for the developers to view a User Story from the perspective of a user (as opposed to system design)
- They aid developers in helping Users to understand/appreciate some development challenges that are usually not very apparent by merely reading a User Story
- They are a great tool for removing confusion and ambiguity on all sides, about what it is

that will ultimately be delivered, and how it should be considered as "Done!"

Keeping in mind how the Agile lifecycle works, no one is suggesting that all of these purposes will be addressed up front - during Product Backlog Planning - when the User Story first enters the scene. However, by the time the story moves from Product to Release to Sprint backlogs, every one of these purposes will have been fulfilled.

6.4 What Do They Look Like?

As discussed earlier, Acceptance criteria really map out the boundaries for developers to use when working on functionality being requested by a User Story. It is those boundaries that will then be tested, in order to validate that the User Story was completed to the users' satisfaction.

Take for instance the following User Story:

As a **Salesperson**,

I want to **be able to enter my Orders quickly**

So that *I can spend more time prospecting for additional orders*

Let's focus on this user's requirement for quick order capture. As a developer, it's very hard to fathom how to build functionality that addresses the need for entering orders "quickly". Equally, once that functionality is developed, it will be similarly difficult for the User to verify whether the tool does, in fact, captures orders "quickly".

To relieve all parties of this dilemma, it would be great if the project team could come up with some specific Acceptance criteria around this requirement. An example could be as follows:

- Orders should be accepted by the system within 1 second after hitting the "Confirm" button
- Static information (Name, Contact# and Address) from prior orders must be brought forward, without me having re-enter it each time an existing customer places a new order

With these Acceptance criteria no clearly articulated, Testers can quickly verify if:

- The system is taking too long (> 1 second) to accept the order
- Previous details (Name, Contact# and Address) are not appearing on new orders

Similarly, when the User tests this to validate if the system works as requested, if either of these tests fails, this particular User Story cannot be classified as "Done". In short, there's no room for ambiguity about what "quickly" means. It's all highlighted in the Acceptance criteria.

SECTION III

7.0 The Approach

In the previous two chapters (Section III, **Chapter 5.0 The Rules** and **Chapter 6.0 Acceptance Criteria**) we gained deep insight into what's needed to build great User Stories. The conclusion was that, if we followed the broad "rules" outlined in Chapter 5.0, and made sure we provided sound Acceptance Criteria (as defined in Chapter 6.0), we would be well on our way to writing highly effective User Stories.

It's now time for us to take a look at a suggested approach, and some techniques, that we can use to put those rules into action.

7.1 Using The Right Approach

Before we discuss one suggested approach to ensuring your User Story is exactly what the project team needs, let's take a moment to recap WHY we are creating User Stories:

> ***We are writing User Stories so that we can accurately and effectively articulate users' requirements***

How we approach this goal will depend entirely upon the comfort-level of the Agile team with the User Story methodology being followed. In **Section II - Ch 2.0 User Stories - The Basics**, we touched upon (at a very high-level) how one can use a User Story Template to capture the essence of the story. Then, in **SECTION III - Ch 5.0 The Rules**, we spoke about how, using an iterative approach, we can progressively flesh out the needs behind each User Story so that the project team (including Users and Techies) get what they need.

We can now put all of that previous learning together and come up with one suggested approach (there may be others that you could use...depending on the experience and comfort level of each team) to User Story creation:

- Since the Product Owner is the voice of the end user, he/she must take it upon himself/herself to connect with all key users and become familiar with the requirements for the project
- During Product Backlog Planning sessions, the project team should brainstorm and come up with a number of Epics (see **section 5.1.1**) that outline the overall project requirements
- Decompose the Epics into further Themes (see **section 5.1.2**), which you can then use for planning Iterations of the project
- When getting ready for a Sprint Backlog Planning session, make sure the component User Stories within each Theme follow all of the rules outlined in **Chapter 5.0**.
- While each component of the User Story Template is essential, of particular value is the **"So that I can..."** piece. A good approach to getting this one right is to insist

that the user provide a short and crisp definition of WHY he/she is asking for the story. If they cannot think of one, or if what they do say doesn't make sense, then it is likely that the story doesn't hold value for the overall project.

- Make especially sure that every story scheduled to be worked upon in a Sprint has corresponding Acceptance Criteria. If they don't, that means the User Story isn't ready to be worked on as yet. Go back to the Product Owner to for more clarity!

When dealing with User Stories for the first time, novice Agile practitioners might be tempted to "finalize" and prioritize every User Story at the start of the project. That is the wrong approach! The good thing about User Stories is that they can be modified, changed and re-prioritized through the Agile project lifecycle. What may have been high-priority as a result of Spring#3, could very well end up becoming low-priority (because some functionality of Sprint#3 has changed priorities) for Sprint#4.

Use the following checklist to guide your approach to User Stories:

Each User Story must be:

- **Complete:** If, after reviewing the entire backlog of stories scheduled in a Release, you find requirements that are still open-ended, you should not go through with those User Stories
- **Testable:** Like the INVEST model discussed in Chapter 5.0 earlier, you should ensure that every requirement outlined by a User Story can be validated with testable scenarios
- **Consistent:** Because of the very iterative nature of the process of creating User Stories, there is a risk that inconsistencies might creep into one or more of them. Before scheduling a User Story for release, make

sure it's requirements do not conflict with other stories in the release

- **User's Perspective:** User Stories should be focusing on the user's perspective of the requirements. Agile teams may use supplementary tools/documentation to detail technical requirements - but that's not how a User Story should be approached. It should be "design free"!
- **Clear:** Do not use "tentative" statements when defining User Stories. Producing them like a "wish list" is the wrong approach. Instead of saying "As a Shipper, <u>it would be great if I can</u>...", say "As a Shipper....<u>I want</u>...."

A good approach to making User Stories highly effective for a project is not to bother going into too much granularity at the beginning - Epics. You'll be wasting your time! Instead, over progressive brainstorming sessions, the true value of each Epic (and its component Themes and User Stories) will emerge. That's when you should deliberate amongst the team to try and prioritize each story.

7.2 User Story Techniques

Now that you have the hang of the right approach to use to build User Stories, it's time to look at some techniques for putting them (User Stories) into productive use.

Start off with a Whiteboard (Storyboard), and draw grid lines as indicated in the picture below.

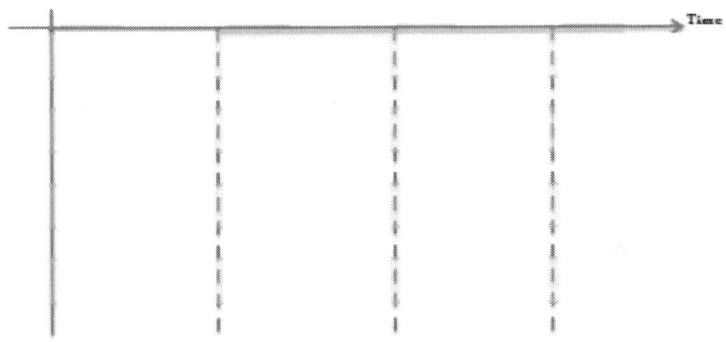

The horizontal axis represents a timeline.

Next, stick all of the Epics at the top of the Storyboard (red squares in the picture below).

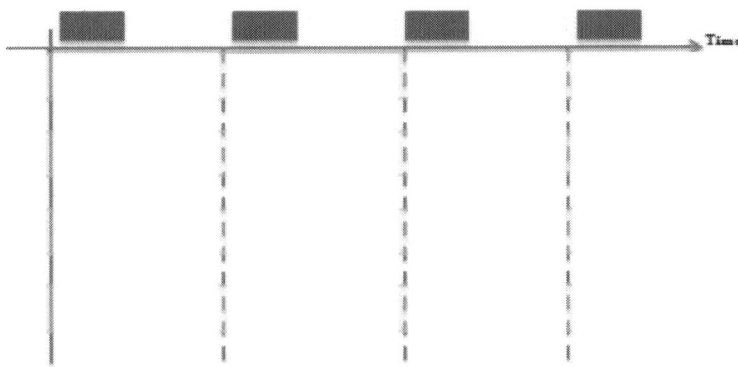

You can now add the number of Releases you envision in the project. Do that to the left of your Storyboard as indicated below:

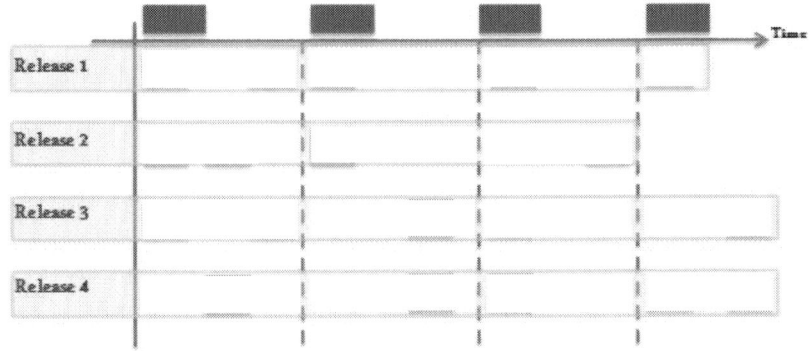

Next, take each of the User Stories and stick them in the grids, under their appropriate Epics. Stories should be arranged side-by-side (horizontally) so that they represent sequential actions required to complete a particular task (feature) - e.g. 1, 2, 3

Copyrights: Axellerata Publishing, 2015 ©

etc. However, if a particular story represents an "or" action (e.g. Users can do 1a or 1b), the stories should be stacked one-on-top-of-another (vertically).

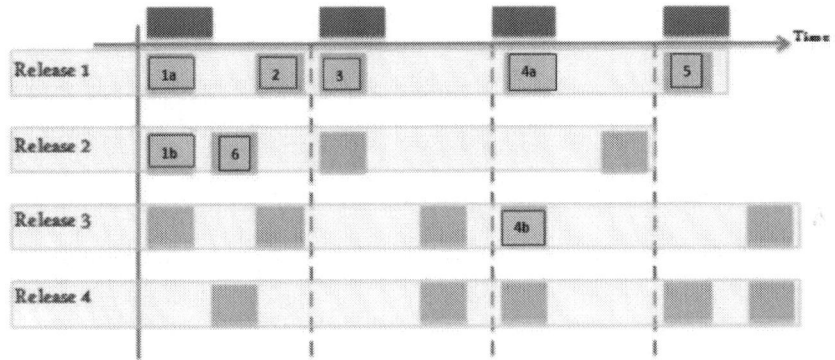

A good technique to determine what User Story should go into which Release is to ask the following question:

- What tasks does the user need to do perform in order to accomplish a certain goal

So, if the answer is: He/she MUST be able to do 1a, 2, 3, 4a and 5 to accomplish the goal, then those are all User Stories that should be released

Copyrights: Axellerata Publishing, 2015 ©

simultaneously. A good technique for scheduling User Stories (in Releases) is:

- Take a look at the Storyboard to see if the sequence of stories currently makes sense
- If they do not, then shift the stories around and brainstorm (with the entire team, including end-users in the process, if required) the merits of the revised sequence
- Do not hesitate to re-arrange the sequence once again (or repeatedly if required) if it makes sense
- Step back, take a look at the re-arranged Storyboard and do a walk-thru of all the stories as they are now lined up for a particular Release once more
- This technique is a great way for the team to quickly spot inconsistencies between related User Stories. E.g.: Why not schedule 1b along with 1a, and push 2 into Release 2?
- Remember, all User Stories do not necessarily need to be scheduled before a

Copyrights: Axellerata Publishing, 2015 ©

Release is planned. There may still be un-prioritized stories left on the Storyboard before the development team starts its work - and that's perfectly okay!

When testing is scheduled, this should be done from left to right. For instance, the first test cycle would include User Stories 1a, 2, 3, 4a and 5. Subsequently, Release 2 testing will include 1b, 6 etc.

Notice that 1a and 1b, and 4a and 4b are in different Releases, and will therefore need to be scheduled in different cycles for testing. That's because the project team will have decided that, for Release 1, the functionality associated with 1a was more important than 1b, and the functionality for 4a was deemed higher priority than that of 4b. Hence User Stories 1a and 4b were scheduled for Release 1, while their corresponding (alternate) stories were scheduled for later releases.

Copyrights: Axellerata Publishing, 2015 ©

Using this technique will ensure that your all of your related User Stories are prioritized and scheduled appropriately.

SECTION III

8.0 Impact of US on Agile Projects

As highlighted a number of times previously in this book, User Stories are written so that they can make a positive impact on a project. Their end objective is to deliver **"value add"** to the user, while aiding the project team in designing, developing and implementing that value-added solution.

In this chapter we'll talk about how Agile teams should use User Stories, throughout a project lifecycle, to make a positive impact on the project.

8.1 Using User Stories in Agile Projects

We can't stress sufficiently that User Stories must be used as they were meant to: To uncover user requirements as articulated by a user. They should

NOT be used as a mere documentation tool - that will defeat the entire purpose of their creation.

```
#SS01 – Story Title [Name of the Story]

    As a ...  [Role / Type of User]


    I need ...  [Feature / Capability]


    So that ...  [Reason / Benefit]
```

SOURCE: Eliassen Group

Some Agile teams use previously created documentation, such as a traditional requirements gathering exercise, to then produce User Stories. Once again, that is a totally incorrect way of using User Stories in Agile settings. Using stories based upon previously created documentation:

- Does not enable User Story to be formatted in the "As a...I need...So that.." template that is highly recommended by Scrum practitioners. Instead, it encourages an overly

Copyrights: Axellerata Publishing, 2015 ©

verbose definition of the story that does not lend itself to an Agile project development process
- Hardly ever ends up framing the User Story from the users' perspective. And that defies one of the chief tenants of the 3C's model - Collaboration! And using a story that does not reflect the perspective of the person or group that owns the story, is a sure recipe for a doomed project!
- Are extremely difficult for the project team to relate to or use effectively, since the original document (e.g. a 50-page Use Case or Requirements Definition Document - RDD) will likely have been produced by a separate team, using a non-Agile methodology

One major benefit of using User Stories in an Agile project environment is that they easily lend themselves to being visually represented and manipulated centrally.

SOURCE: Eliassen Group

Users as well as project team members can view the story, plastered across a wall or a whiteboard, and can alter their sequence and prioritization during Scrum sessions. This is a great way for brainstorming, using User Stories to crystalize a proposed sequence of events that will ultimately lead to a solution that everyone on the team owns - not just a select few indivudials who may have authored a RDD or Use Case.

8.2 User Story Lifecycle

Readers may rightfully ask: Why have you delayed discussing this topic- User Story Lifecycle - until now. Shouldn't this have been the very first topic to be covered? Not really! We deliberately delayed discussing this topic until now, because now that you have a clear understanding of what User Stories are, What value they bring and how they work, you can truly begin to appreciate how they evolve in an Agile project setting.

Agile is an iterative methodology that believes in delivering value-add in small, progressive, increments throughout a project's lifecycle. And User Stories fit that methodology perfectly. Why? Because like the Agile methodology itself, User Stories evolve throughout the lifecycle of the project.

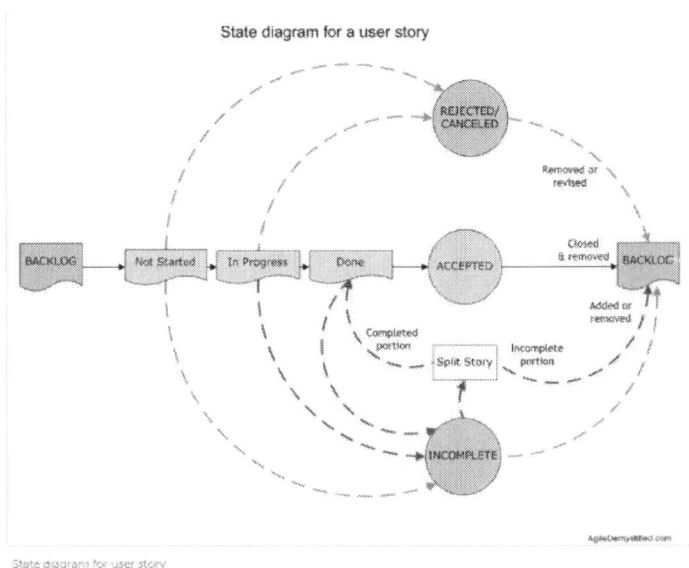

State diagram for user story

Just as various deliverables of an Agile project, for example a software application, evolve throughout the project, until the last piece of code is written, tested and implemented, so too the details of a User Story are not complete - until they are! That sounds like a very flip statement, but it's true.

8.2.1 Evolution of User Stories

User Stories are constantly reviewed and updated throughout the project's planning horizon. And the nearer a User Story is to being worked on (possibly for inclusion in the next release), the more details are known about it. Therefore, in general terms, the lifecycle of a User Story can be defined in the following sequence:

- The project team will likely know much more about a User Story that is planned for inclusion in Release 1, than one that's scheduled for Release 5
- By the time the team has delivered Release 4, the team will know everything there is to know about all User Stories scheduled for Release 5, but may not know too much about the ones planned for Release 7

Like everything else in an Agile project, this iterative evolution of User Stories has a purpose. It's no use decomposing stories that are further down the time horizon, than say one or two releases out. Things could change in releases prior to that, which may mean changing everything you did to those (distant) User Stories - something that project teams with limited resources want to avoid.

8.2.2 User Stories State

User Stories take on a particular "state" as they evolve throughout their lifecycle. That's because, at any given point in their lives, the project team is either not doing anything to them (which leaves their status unchanged), or are doing something to them which transform their status.

- **Backlog:** All User Stories that have been approved (in principle) to be worked upon, get assigned into the Backlog queue
- **Not Started:** By default therefore, all User Stories get assigned a status of "Not Started" because no work has been done on them as yet
- **In Progress:** As the Backlogged stories are prioritized and released to the team to work upon, the status of those stories changes from "Not Started" into "In Progress". User Stories are worked upon in terms of the priority that's assigned to them. So usually, you should expect to see several stories on

the Storyboard whose statuses are "In Progress"

- **Done:** When the project team has developed and tested the User Story, and is ready to have it presented at the next Sprint review, the status changes from "In Progress" into "Done". It is important for readers to remember what the definition of "Done" is. "Done" represents the ability for the developed solution to meet all of the Acceptance criteria set out for it. This is in keeping with the "Confirmation" pillar of the 3C's model

- **Accepted:** During Sprint reviews, the development team demonstrates the features/functionality created to the Product Owner (and other team members). If the PO determines that he/she is satisfied with the demonstration, the story will be marked as "Accepted". When that happens, the User Story is removed from the Backlog queue

- **Incomplete:** Should the developed functionality fail to meet the predetermined acceptance criteria during Sprint review, the story will be marked as "Incomplete". The choices then faced by the team might include:

    - Rescheduling the User Story for the next Sprint
    - Re-prioritizing it for a future Release
    - Changing the story, splitting it or reviewing the underlying basis for its existence

    User Stories might also be marked as "Incomplete" because of upstream defects that they may have introduced into previously working functionality.

- **Rejected/Cancelled:** If, as a result of Sprint review, it is determined that the User Story is no longer required, it will be flagged as

"Cancelled'. Alternately, a User Story still in "Not Started" or "In Progress" status, or that was previously "Done", can also be designated as "Cancelled" if the PO determines that it has no value to the project anymore

Cancelled/Rejected User Stories could have both upstream and downstream impacts to a project's lifecycle, because the team could potentially have to review prioritization of stories scheduled for future iterations, or even need to "undo" previously "done" functionality as a result of cancellations.

The most important take-away from this discussion is to remember that User Stories have an evolutionary lifecycle that they must go through. Just like an ugly-looking larva evolves into a beautiful-looking butterfly, so too highly-effective User Stories can evolve from sketchy and often vague Epics. The iterative process of the Agile methodology ensures that User Story lifecycles take a rough-cut stone and polish it into a perfect gem!

SECTION III

9.0 Doing it right - Tips & Tricks

When working in an Agile Project environment, time is of essence. What that means is, the project team has a limited amount of time in which to complete a Sprint, and there is also a finite amount of time allocated for each Release. "Messing" it up will have ripple effects on following Releases and subsequent Sprints within the current Release.

So why was it necessary to repeat this very obvious impact on timelines? Because it's important to highlight the need to get your User Stories right - or else risk project derailment!

9.1 Why Do It Right?

User Stories are the central tool used in Agile projects to capture, define and refine value-add to meet user requirements. And since those requirements are what the project is all about, it behoves the Agile team to make sure they nail the User Stories behind the requirements right.

THINK QUALITY!

DO IT RIGHT THE FIRST TIME
WE DON'T ALWAYS GET A SECOND CHANCE

SOURCE: Seton.Net.Au

In an earlier discussion in the book we talked about the repetitive nature of defining and refining User Stories. It is that precise repetitiveness that makes it all the more important for Agile practitioners to get User Stories right - the very first time! Why? Because:

- Incorrectly defined User Stories included in the Product Backlog will start a chain of unwanted events
- They may be incorrectly prioritized and included into a Release Backlog

- Which will then cause them to be (wrongly!) prioritized and addressed, as work steps in the Sprint Backlog

Ultimately, because the team got the User Story wrong the first time (during Product Backlog Planning), the impact will cascade all the way down to delivering an incorrect feature/functionality in a Sprint deliverable.

9.2 How To Do It Right?

Here are a few tips and tricks that creators of User Stories can use to ensure they get it right the first time!

1) **Make it about Users:** Many technical team members have an instant desire to think of user requirements in terms of "system functionality" or "application features". That mentality is a sure way of getting User Stories wrong - every time! The trick is to make the user the focus of the User Story. They should be written from his/her

(user's) perspective, and not a Developer or System Architect's perspective

2) **Personify it:** The goal of creating a User Story is to try and help the team understand the "pain point" that is being addressed by the story, so that the most appropriate solution to it can be developed. To understand that "pain", you must use personas in your stories. By creating User Stories around the needs of personas, such as "Customer", "Supervisor", "Shipper", you can better highlight the value-added needs of the system, than by focusing on abstract users - such as "Management" or "Users of the system"

3) **Collaborate on it:** As highlighted earlier on in the book, a User Story is not a requirement definition document, nor is it meant to be a system specification. It is meant to be a line item on a "To Do" list for the team, which says "Hey...we need to discuss this User Story next".

Copyrights: Axellerata Publishing, 2015 ©

As such, User Stories must be developed collaboratively, in consultation with the Product Owner, Product Users and the Project Team

4) **Keep it simple!** This is one of the most important tips for getting User Stories right. Earlier on in this book, readers got a glimpse of a User Story Template. Use that template as your guide when creating each story, and:
   - Keep It simple (KIS)!
   - Keep it concise!
   - Keep it unambiguous!
   - Use easy to understand language

5) **Break it up!** During the Product Planning stage, it is possible that some User Stories will start off as high-level Epics - which paint a broad picture of the requirement. These then need to be further reviewed and refined into smaller, more detailed User Stories. The objective is to take the Epic, and break it down to a level where it

can be "actioned" (converted into a doable task), and tested.

6) **Keep it visible!** Since collaboration and communication are hallmarks of successful User Story creation, it goes without saying that the status of those stories needs to be put on open display for everyone on the team to access and view - at all times.

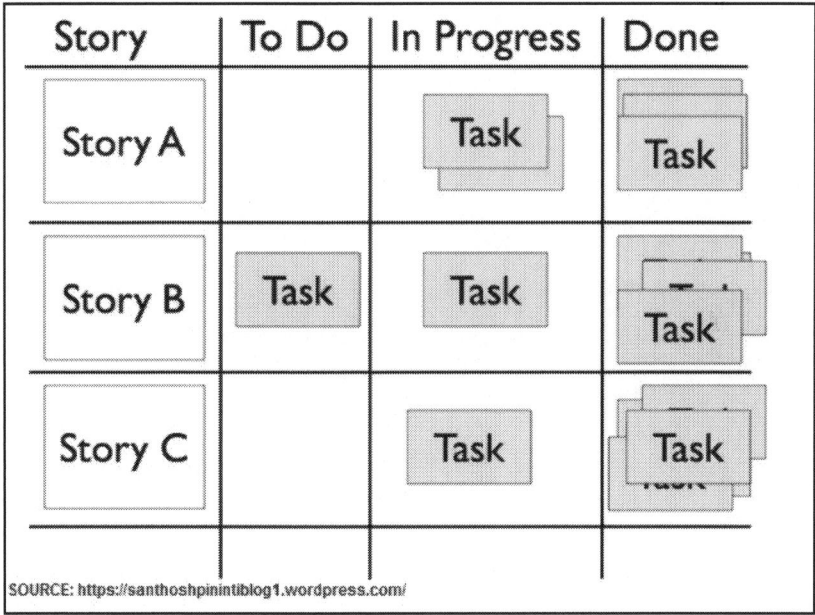

Using a User Storyboard that's in a central location, say on a whiteboard or a wall, is a great way to ensure both accessibility and visibility

7) **Validate it!** A well written User Story is only half complete if it cannot be validated. And that's where Acceptance criteria come in. Because the User Story will become part of the features/functionality of the system being delivered, it has to be validated during testing. Without well thought out Acceptance criteria associated with the User Story, neither Product Owners or users, nor the project team will be able to validate whether the requirement highlighted by the story was successfully addressed

8) **Supplement it - where possible:** Since User Stories are, by definition, concise and succinct "reminders" of a task that needs to be completed, they are by nature not an all-

inclusive description of what actually needs to be done to execute the User Story. Therefore, where necessary, the project team should consider supplementing each User Story with additi`onal information, in the form of User Journeys, Visual Design documentation and Functional Specifications.

SECTION IV

10.0 Samples & Examples

We've come a long way now, since we first introduced User Stories to you. Over the course of various discussions in this book, you've learned how User Stories evolved as a tool for requirements gathering. You've also gained a good understanding of what they can do (value add) for Agile projects, and you've got a good understanding of the "rules", conventions and best practices for developing them.

It's now time to put all of that knowledge together into a small, yet compact, example of how to build good User Stories.

10.1 Introducing the Salesperson

For the purpose of this example, let's revive our hypothetical Salesperson (see **Section 2.1.2** for reference). Further, let's assume that the logistics company Speedy Logistics Ltd. has decided to go ahead with a project to build a system that will help its staff expedite customer order processing and shipping.

A detailed discussion about why this particular project would have been chosen, and how various components of the system will be delivered, is out of the scope of this book. For a better understanding of how the entire project would have been managed, see my previous publication: *Project Management: A Compact Guide to the Complex World of Project Management*.

Speedy Logistics Ltd. employs several staff, including Salespeople, Shippers, and Supervisors. For the purpose of our User Story example however, we will focus on a few requirements that the Shipping department believes need to be addressed by the new system.

Our example also assumes that Speedy Logistics' management has chosen to use an Agile project management methodology, and have organized the project team with the appropriate roles (Scrum Master, Product Owner, Scrum Team members). Once again, a detailed discussion of Scrum and various project roles is beyond the scope of this book. It is highly recommended that, to make effective use of User Stories (the focus of this book), readers should get a strong grounding on Scrum by reading my earlier publication - <u>Scrum: Your Quick Start Guide To Adopting Scrum For Your Organization</u>.

10.2 The Salespersons' Stories

One of the first people that the project team discusses requirements with is Sally, one of the Salespeople on the team.

10.2.1 User Story 001.00 - Customer Order Processing

When the project team started discussing the requirements of the Salesperson, Sally, she initially said that Customer Order Processing was her primary requirement. As a result, the project team was able to create their first User Story, which was documented on an Index Card as follows:

User Story#	:	001.00
User Story Title	:	Customer Order Processing
As a	:	Salesperson
I want to	:	Confirm customer orders quickly
So that	:	I can receive commission credits faster

ACCEPTANCE CRITERIA

1) Salesperson should be able to log-in from the main menu - No more than 5 to 7 seconds
2) 'View Your Order's Queue' should be the first option available to select
3) Pending order status must be highlighted in bold, red font
4) Allowable pending order status codes - Incomplete (INC) ; On hold (HOL) ; Rejected (REJ) ; Confirmed (CON)
5) Status changes should take no more than 3 seconds to get updated

Recall from all our previous discussions, the User Story must be the "voice of the user", and that's exactly what the team did - they let Sally tell them exactly WHAT she needs (...to Confirm customer orders quickly) and WHY (so she can receive commission credits faster).

When this User Story is discussed in detail, the project team will have asked Sally the following questions:

Team: Can you further explain the word "quickly" for us?

Sally: I should be able to log in from the main menu within 5 to 7 seconds - the current system takes ages to log in! And I shouldn't need to hunt around for the option to view all of my Orders - that'll only slow down the confirmation process. Also, once I'm done, it should not take more than 3 seconds for me to save my updates. The existing system takes 5 minutes some days!

Note: If we take a look at Acceptance Criteria 1), 2) and 5), the User Story captures all that Sally has said, but very succinctly and concisely. All other nonessential discussions were filtered out from the story.

Team: How will you be able to quickly confirm your orders once you see them?

Sally: Well, if there was some way that I could immediately see what the current status is, then I could quickly change it appropriately and confirm the order.

Team: What do you mean by "appropriately"?

Sally: Well, if I notice that there's something missing from the order, I must be able to flag it as incomplete; or if there is some other issue, I must be able to put the order on hold; I must also have the option to reject the order if this is a customer with a bad history, and I don't want to deal with him/her. Otherwise, I must have the ability to simply change the status to "Confirmed" and be done!

Note: How succinctly the User Story has captured this entire requirement using Acceptance Criteria 3) and 4).

While the team listened patiently to Sally's verbose description of what she needs and why, just the facts (summarized, of course!) were captured on the Index Card, making it a prime sample of how User Stories are produced. However, we're not yet done!

One of the developers on the team was also taking notes as Sally spoke (BTY: there's no law that says you're not allowed to transcribe a User Story session and keep those notes for future reference - as happened in this case!). He noted that Sally spoke about "history"...and the following Q&A session ensued:

Team: Sally, a minute ago you said *"I must also have the option to reject the order if this is a customer with a bad history, and I don't want to deal with him/her."* So, how do you intend to do that - i.e. decide if you should reject the client's order?

Sally: Well, that's another story (Sally jokes!). We usually don't like to entertain orders from customers with repeated issues. So, I need to be able to see if the customer has a good history with

Copyrights: Axellerata Publishing, 2015 ©

us, or if he/she has had problems (either with me or other Salespeople on the team), and that will help me decide if I want to accept or reject the order.

Note: Another story indeed! Sally hit the nail on the head. This is definitely "another story", because it deals with a different (albeit related) set of requirements.

So, the project team regroups and discusses what this new revelation means for Story 001.00 - Customer Order Processing. They could go back and start modifying it to add additional verbiage to the "So that I" component, and also expanding the Acceptance Criteria. However, that would fly in the face of our basic 3C's building blocks that we had previously discussed (see **Section 4.1 Illustrative Building Blocks**). Instead, following good User Story development guidelines, the team decided to create another User Story to deal with this requirement.

10.2.2 User Story 002.00 - Customer History Look-up

The project team now knew that, for Sally to work efficiently, she needed access to customer history. So the team started discussing how the system could add more value for Sally in order to give her what she needs:

Team: Sally, tell us more about this need to view customer history.

Sally: Well, I know all of my exclusive customers pretty well...so most of the time I can just confirm their orders without looking to see if they've paid their invoices. But some customers also place orders with other Salespeople, and I need to quickly check their history on the fly. I don't want to have to call someone to ask about this customer. I should have some way of doing it right as I'm viewing my orders.

After several other follow-up questions, the team is able to narrow down exactly what Sally needs to be able to fulfil this requirement.

User Story#	:	002.00
User Story Title	:	Customer History Look-up

As a	:	Salesperson
I want to	:	Review a customers' History
So that	:	I can decide whether to accept or decline his/her order

ACCEPTANCE CRITERIA

1) Ability to access 'View Customer History' for every order in the Order queue by clicking 'View History' button
2) History screen should pop-up in current window (NOT a new window)
3) Ability to show/hide history by toggling between views

Notice how the Acceptance criteria takes Sally's words like "quickly", "on the fly" and "right as I'm viewing", and converts them into specific actions that the system should demonstrate so that it receives Sally's approval during Sprint review.

10.2.3 User Story 002.A & B - Customer Order/Payment History Look-up

When the team regrouped to discuss how this latest User story will unfold, the scribe noticed that there was more to the term "history" than met the eye. They decided to query Sally further:

Copyrights: Axellerata Publishing, 2015 ©

Team: So Sally, tell us what you meant by "history". You talk about knowing if customers "...pay their invoices", and you also talk about "...place orders with other Salespeople". So what exactly do you want in terms of history?

Sally: Actually, I need to see both how well a customer has paid in the past, as well as the volume of orders they place with the company - not just with me. Sometimes, bulk customers are allowed additional orders, even if they have one or two invoices outstanding. The company knows they will settle the invoices shortly.

Well, this is now all beginning to make sense. Sally has now told the team everything she needs for her to be able to quickly log on, view her order queue, check a customer's order and payment history, and quickly confirm or reject an order. But this has created a slight bit of debate within the team.

- Should they create just a single User Story for Sally's "Customer Order and Payment

History Look-up" requirement, or should they split them up into two separate User Stories

Recalling all our previous discussions, we see that User Stories should be Independent, they should be Concise, and they should be Testable. Squeezing the requirement to do both Order and Payment look-ups through a single story-point would make the story large and "tied together". The team therefore decided to split this requirement into two User Stories as follows:

User Story#	:	002.A
User Story Title	:	Customer Order History Look-up
As a	:	Salesperson
I want to	:	Review a customers' Order History
So that	:	I can decide whether to accept or decline his/her order based on volume of past orders
ACCEPTANCE CRITERIA		
1) Ability to access 'View Customer History' for every order in the Order queue by clicking 'View History - Orders' button
2) History screen should pop-up in current window (NOT a new window)
3) Ability to show/hide history by toggling between views		

User Story#	:	002.B
User Story Title	:	Customer Payment History Look-up

As a	:	Salesperson
I want to	:	Review a customers' Payment History
So that	:	I can decide whether to accept or decline his/her order based on past order payments

ACCEPTANCE CRITERIA

1) Ability to access 'View Customer History' for every order in the Order queue by clicking 'View History - Payments' button
2) History screen should pop-up in current window (NOT a new window)
3) Ability to show/hide history by toggling between views

With these two User Stories defined separately:

- They can be prioritized independently
- They can each be scheduled in the same (or separate releases)
- They can be tested and verified separately
- Issues in deploying one (002.A Customer Order History Look-up) should have no impact on delivering the other (002.B Customer Payment History Look-up)

And that's exactly how a good User Story should be constructed.

Copyrights: Axellerata Publishing, 2015 ©

10.3 The End Of Storytelling

The above example should give you an excellent idea of how to go about decomposing high-level user requirements into more granular User Stories. We have used all of the building blocks and all of the best practices, discussed throughout the book, in developing our 4 samples above. In real life however, you are likely to end up with dozens of such stories - not just three or four - to deal with typical user requirements.

Also, while it may seem like these 4 sample stories evolved over the course of single interaction with Sally, reality is far from it. Coming up with just these 4 User Stories may take a few hours, a few days, or might span the entire project timeline. It all depends on how complex the requirements are, how many stories they span over, and how many Releases/iterations a project comprises of.

Copyrights: Axellerata Publishing, 2015 ©

SECTION IV

11.0 Tools & Products

11.1 Useful Links

The following are useful links that readers may find helpful when defining, refining and managing User Stories on their projects. While some of these tools have broader application in Agile/Scrum project environments, all of them have at least some aspect of User Stories embedded in them.

Tool	Vendor	License	Application type
StoriesOnBoard	DevMads Ltd.	Commercial, Free	Browser
BacklogTool	Sony Mobile Communications	Free	Browser
SonicAgile - FREE Agile Project Management Tool	SonicAgile	Free	Browser
Scrumwise	Scrumwise	Commercial	Browser
Yodiz	Yodiz	Commercial, Free	Browser, IDE Plugin
Eylean Board	Prewise UAB	Commercial	Native, TFS Plugin
engile	engile	Commercial,	Browser

Copyrights: Axellerata Publishing, 2015 ©

		Free	
WorkEngine	EPM Live	Commercial	Browser, TFS Plugin
easyBacklog	easyBacklog	Commercial, Free	Browser
Agilo for Scrum	Agilo Software powered by agile42	Commercial	Browser
ScrumHalf	GPE Ltda.	Commercial, Free	Browser
ScrumDo	ScrumDo LLC	Commercial, Free	Browser
Redmine Backlogs	Redmine Backlogs	Free	Browser
tinyPM	Agilers	Commercial, Free	Browser
Select Scope Manager	Select Business Solutions	Commercial	Browser
Sprintometer v6.50	Sprintometer Ltd.	Free	Native
Rally Community Edition	Rally Software Development	Free	Browser
Rally Enterprise Edition	Rally Software Development	Commercial	Browser
VersionOne	VersionOne	Commercial	Browser
ProjectCards	ProjeNova	Commercial, Free	IDE Plugin, Native
ScrumPad	Code71	Commercial	Browser
Agilo for trac	Agilo Software powered by agile42	Free	Browser
ScrumDesk	ScrumDesk	Commercial, Free	IDE Plugin, Native, Other, TFS Plugin
Courtesy: http://www.userstories.com/products			

Copyrights: Axellerata Publishing, 2015 ©

Some of the tools listed above offer free versions of the tool, albeit with somewhat restricted functionality. It may be prudent to give those limited-functionality versions a try first, before forming an opinion on whether the tool is suited to an individual reader's needs.

11.2 Disclaimer

Readers should note that the inclusion of a product/tool in this list in no way construes a recommendation. These links have been provided only by way of information, and these products have not been evaluated for technical or functional fit. Readers should use them only after conducting appropriate diligence and their own "fit for use" assessment.

Printed in Great Britain
by Amazon.co.uk, Ltd.,
Marston Gate.